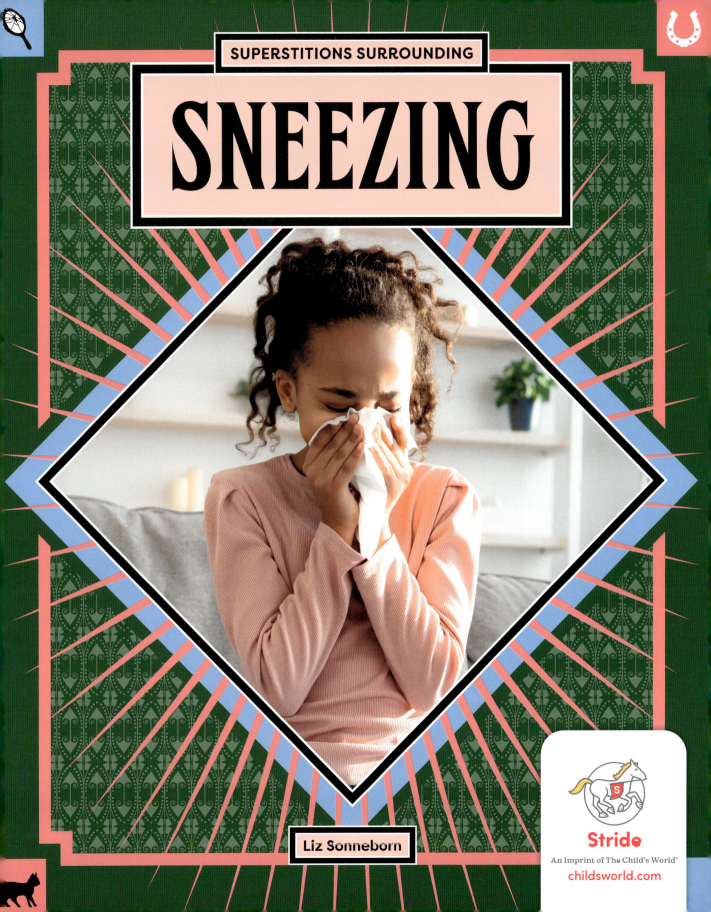

Published by The Child's World®
800-599-READ • childsworld.com

Copyright © 2023 by The Child's World®
All rights reserved. No part of this book may be reproduced or utilized in any form or by any means without written permission from the publisher.

Photography Credits
Photographs ©: Prostock Studio/Shutterstock Images, cover, 1, 6; Light Field Studios/Shutterstock Images, 5; iStockphoto, 9, 21; Dragana Gordic/Shutterstock Images, 10, 16; Mikhail Markovskiy/Shutterstock Images, 11; Ann Rodchua/Shutterstock Images, 13; Shutterstock Images, 14, 17; Elena Rui/Shutterstock Images, 19

ISBN Information
9781503865136 (Reinforced Library Binding)
9781503866478 (Portable Document Format)
9781503867314 (Online Multi-user eBook)
9781503868151 (Electronic Publication)

LCCN 2022939699

Printed in the United States of America

About the Author

A graduate of Swarthmore College, Liz Sonneborn has written more than 100 books for young readers and adults. Her specialties include U.S. history, world history, biographies, women's studies, and African American studies.

CONTENTS

CHAPTER ONE
Achoo! . . . 4

CHAPTER TWO
The Dangerous Sneeze . . . 8

CHAPTER THREE
Around the World . . . 12

CHAPTER FOUR
Making a Connection . . . 18

Glossary . . . 22

Fast Facts . . . 23

One Stride Further . . . 23

Find Out More . . . 24

Index . . . 24

CHAPTER ONE

ACHOO!

It starts with a tickling in a person's nose. Her breathing gets quicker, her chest tightens, and her eyes close. Suddenly, air and spit spew from her nose and mouth as she lets out a big sneeze. Without even thinking, a person nearby says "bless you." Reciting this simple phrase after someone sneezes is an old **superstition**.

> Sneezes can travel up to 100 miles per hour (161 kmh). They can contain around 40,000 droplets of spit. These droplets can stay in the air for several minutes.

Sneezes can be caused by allergies, sickness, or something getting into a person's nose.

> *A sneeze can travel more than 6 feet (1.8 m). That is why it is important for people to cover their mouths when they sneeze.*

Sneezes are natural and common. A sneeze is the body's way of keeping a dangerous **irritant** out of the body. The irritant might be a **germ**, dust, pollen, smoke, or even perfume.

So why do some people feel the need to say a **blessing** for someone who sneezes? After all, no one says "bless you" after hearing a cough or a burp. The answer comes from centuries of unfounded fears about the act of sneezing.

CHAPTER TWO

THE DANGEROUS SNEEZE

There are a few explanations for why people say "bless you" after a sneeze. Some ancient **philosophers** believed that a person's soul was located in the head. They thought a sneeze could **expel** the soul from the body. Saying "bless you" was a way to ask God to save the sneezer's soul.

Some Hindus also feared evil spirits. They thought spirits could enter the body through the nose during a sneeze. Saying a blessing was a way of stopping this. Other people thought sneezes could release evil spirits. In this case, a blessing was meant to protect the sneezer from spirits reentering his or her body. The blessing was also said to protect people close to the sneezer.

In the 1600s, French philosopher René Descartes believed that the soul was in the brain.

Most people today do not think sneezes and evil spirits are connected, but they may not want to be around someone who seems sick.

Sneezing increases pressure in the chest. This can slightly interrupt blood flow to the heart. As a result, it may feel like the heart skips a beat. This sensation led to the **myth** that a sneeze stops the heart. In this case, the blessing was a request to God to bring the sneezer back to life.

In the 500s, a **plague** struck the city of Rome. This illness was often deadly. A sneeze was frequently the first sign that someone had the plague. Pope Gregory I was the head of the Catholic Church. He told his Roman followers to say "God bless you" when someone sneezed.

He believed that the blessing could help the sneezer escape death.

All these ideas about sneezes might seem strange now. But before modern medicine, sneezes could be frightening. No one knew when a sneeze might be a sign of a serious illness. Long ago, asking a higher power for help made sense to many people. It seemed like their only defense against the dangers of a sneeze.

Saying "God bless you" was meant to be a prayer to God to keep people healthy. Pope Gregory I started this to try and comfort people during the plague.

CHAPTER THREE
AROUND THE WORLD

People in many countries have their own expressions for addressing individuals after a sneeze. For instance, people in Islamic countries say *yarhamuk Allah*. This means "God's blessing" in Arabic.

Often, words said after someone sneezes are merely wishes for good health. Germans say *gesundheit*. Italians say *salute*. Spanish speakers say *salud*. These words all mean "health." Russians say *bud zdorov* to adults. That means "be healthy." But to children, they also say *rosti bolshoi*, which means "grow big."

There are a lot of responses to sneezes from all over the world about wishing the sneezer good health.

In Mexico, if a person sneezes one time people respond with salud, *twice* dinero, *and three times* amor. *This translates to* health, money, *and* love. *They believe these things make for a happy life.*

The Chinese do things a little differently. In China, no one says anything to a person after he sneezes. However, the sneezer is expected to excuse himself for making so much noise.

People from different countries also have their own old sneezing superstitions. According to a popular Polish belief, a sneeze means that a person's mother-in-law is saying bad things about him or her. Traditionally, Scottish parents were eager for their baby's first sneeze. It was said to release the child from a fairy's spell. In Italy, people were excited whenever a cat sneezed. It was a sign that good luck was coming their way.

> A 12-year-old girl named Donna Griffiths holds the all-time sneezing record. She sneezed every few minutes for 977 days straight.

In Iran, if a person sneezes while making a decision, it is a sign that he or she should not go ahead with it.

A Japanese superstition states that the number of times a person sneezes can mean different things. If people sneeze once, someone will compliment them. If they sneeze twice, someone will speak badly of them. People who sneeze three times are destined to have someone laugh at them. Four sneezes means the person is getting a cold.

CHAPTER FOUR

MAKING A CONNECTION

Today, people know that sneezes can spread germs. To prevent this, people often use tissues to cover their mouths and noses when they sneeze, or they sneeze into their sleeves. Many people no longer fear that sneezes will expel their souls or expose them to evil spirits.

Yet many people still say "bless you" whenever they hear a sneeze. Some people do it without thinking. They say the phrase simply out of habit. Others were taught from childhood that they must say "bless you." They believe it is the polite thing to do.

There is no proof that a sneeze will harm a person's soul, but sneezes can be unlucky for people nearby if the sneezer is sick.

There is no scientific evidence that saying anything after a sneeze will actually help a person. Yet there is one practical reason many people still say this: it may make them feel good. When they say "bless you," some people believe they are offering a small kindness to another person. When people hear that phrase, they may take it as a sign that someone cares about their health.

Between 18 and 35 percent of people have a photic sneeze reflex. That means they often sneeze when they are suddenly exposed to bright light.

Believing in superstitions helps some people reduce stress and feel more in control of their lives.

Some superstitions about sneezing have survived for hundreds of years. Blessing a sneezer is unlikely to disappear anytime soon. Perhaps as long as there are sneezes, there will people who say "bless you."

GLOSSARY

blessing (BLES-ing) A blessing is a prayer asking for help or protection from a god. People sometimes offer a blessing when they hear someone sneeze.

expel (ek-SPEL) To expel means to force out. Sneezes expel air from the sneezer's lungs.

germ (JERM) A germ is a tiny thing that can cause a disease. A sneeze is one way the body tries to get rid of a germ.

irritant (EER-uh-tant) An irritant is something that causes discomfort in the body. Dust is an irritant that can make a person sneeze.

myth (MITH) A myth is a common but false belief. It is a myth that evil spirits can enter the body during a sneeze.

philosophers (fuh-LOSS-uh-furs) Philosophers are people who study basic questions about life. Some ancient philosophers thought a person's soul was in the head.

plague (PLAYG) A plague is a disease that spreads quickly and infects and kills a lot of people. Long ago, a sneeze was an early sign that someone had a plague.

superstition (soo-pur-STIH-shuhn) A superstition is a belief that certain events cause good or bad luck. The superstition surrounding saying "bless you" after a sneeze is common in many places.

FAST FACTS

- In ancient times, people believed a sneeze could allow evil spirits to enter the body.

- In the 500s, Pope Gregory I told his followers to say "God bless you" when someone sneezed to protect that person from illness.

- In some cultures, people wish a sneezer good health rather than saying "bless you."

- Many people say "bless you" after a sneeze out of habit or to be polite.

ONE STRIDE FURTHER

- Have you ever said "bless you" after someone sneezed? If so, why did you do it?

- Why do you think different cultures have different superstitions surrounding sneezing?

- Do you think saying a phrase like "bless you" to someone is more helpful or harmful? Explain your answer.

FIND OUT MORE

IN THE LIBRARY

Favor, Lesli J., and Margaux Baum. *Bacteria*. New York, NY: Rosen Central, 2017.

Levine, Sara. *Germs Up Close*. Minneapolis, MN: Millbrook Press, 2021.

Rose, Rachel. *Sneeze*. Minneapolis, MN: Bearport, 2023.

ON THE WEB

Visit our website for links about sneezing:
childsworld.com/links

Note to Parents, Teachers, and Librarians: We routinely verify our Web links to make sure they are safe and active sites. So encourage your readers to check them out!

INDEX

blessing, 7, 8, 10–11, 12, 21

China, 14

germ, 7

Hindus, 8

irritant, 7

Japanese, 17

philosophers, 8

plague, 10

Roman, 10

spirits, 8, 18